GW00645199

Inspire Books is an imprint of
Peter Pauper Press, Inc.

For permissions please see the
last page of this book.

Text copyright © 1999
Peter Pauper Press, Inc.
202 Mamaroneck Avenue
White Plains, NY 10601
Illustrations copyright © 1999
Kerren Barbas
All rights reserved
ISBN 0-88088-133-X
Printed in China
7 6 5 4 3 2 1

Joy to the world! the Lord is come;

Let earth receive her King;

Let every heart prepare Him room,

And heav'n and nature sing,

And heav'n and nature sing,

And heav'n, and heav'n, and nature sing.

Isaac Watts,
Joy to the World

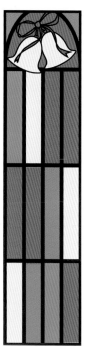

And the angel said unto them, Fear not: for, behold, I bring you good tidings of great joy, which shall be to all people. For unto you is born this day in the city of David a Savior, which is Christ the Lord.

Luke 2:10-11 KJV

The wonder of Christmas is its simplicity. . . . There are the shepherds—the first Christmas congregation. Humble folks, these, folks who lived close to the things God made—the earth the carpet for their feet, the sun and stars their coverings.

Harriett Thatcher

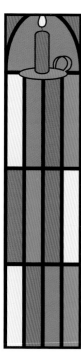

What can I give Him
Poor as I am?
If I were a shepherd,
I would give Him a lamb,
If I were a Wise Man,
I would do my part,—
But what I can I give Him,
Give my heart.

Christina G. Rossetti

The way to Christmas lies through an ancient gate. It is a little gate, child-high, child-wide, and there is a password: "Peace on earth to men of good will." May you, this Christmas, become as a little child again and enter into His kingdom.

Angelo Patri

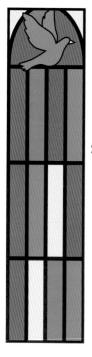

$\mathcal{A}$nd she will bring forth a
Son, and you shall call His name
Jesus, for He will save
His people from their sins.

Matthew 1:21 NKJV

This Child is sent to fill thine heart, and for no other reason is He born. And when the heart thus gives itself up through faith, it finds what His name is, namely this: "sweet Jesus."

Martin Luther

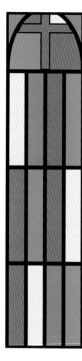

$\mathcal{I}$f we could condense

all the truths of Christmas

into only three words,

these would be the words:

"God with us."

John F. MacArthur, Jr.

He who has not

Christmas in his heart

will never find it under a tree.

Roy L. Smith

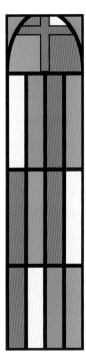

I am so glad He was not born
In some rich palace bed.
I am so glad to know it was
A lowly place, instead,
A place where soft-eyed cows and sheep
Were sheltered and were fed.

And so I like to think of Him,
First opening His eyes
In that good elemental place
Beneath the friendly skies,
That the men of fields could find Him there,
As well as the great and wise.

Grace Noll Crowell

The Bethlehem story
may be familiar, but it should
never be commonplace.
It is a glorious reminder of the
coming of a Child, the King,
our Savior. Rejoice!

For unto us a child is born,
unto us a son is given:
and the government shall be
upon his shoulder: and his name
shall be called Wonderful,
Counsellor, The mighty God,
The everlasting Father, The
Prince of Peace.

Isaiah 9:6 KJV

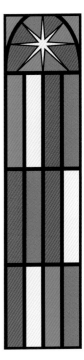

He will be great and will be called the Son of the Most High. The Lord God will give him the throne of his father David . . .

Luke 1:32 NIV

Christ's gift was love;

His mission, release.

His promise was life;

Christ's legacy, peace.

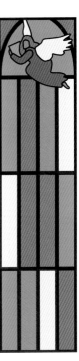

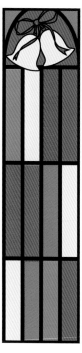

Church bells ring; cash registers clang; voices sing; glasses clink in toasts of good cheer. All these are the sounds of Christmas.

Yet the first sound of Christmas was a gentle sound, a hushed sound, a life-changing sound— a baby's cry in a small stable in Bethlehem.

There's a song in the air,

There's a star in the sky;

There's a mother's deep prayer

And a Baby's low cry;

And the star rains its fire where

the Beautiful sing,

For the manger at Bethlehem

cradles a King.

Josiah G. Holland

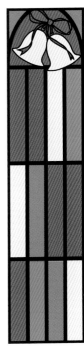

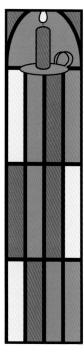

$\mathcal{A}$nd she brought forth her
firstborn Son, and wrapped
Him in swaddling cloths,
and laid Him in a manger,
because there was no room
for them in the inn.

Luke 2:7 NKJV

If Joseph had lacked faith to trust God or humility to perceive the holiness of his spouse, he could have disbelieved in the miraculous origin of her Son as easily as any modern man; and any modern man who believes in God can accept the miracle as easily as Joseph did.

C. S. Lewis

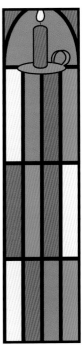

Away in a manger, no crib for a bed,

The little Lord Jesus laid down His sweet head;

The stars in the bright sky

looked down where He lay,

The little Lord Jesus asleep on the hay.

The cattle are lowing, the Baby awakes,

But little Lord Jesus, no crying He makes.

I love Thee, Lord Jesus,

look down from the sky,

And stay by my cradle till morning is nigh.

Unknown

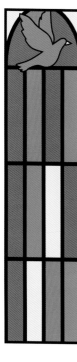

May you find the peace

of the shepherds

And the joy of the angel's song;

As the precious Child

of Bethlehem

Guides you now

and all year long.

Amen.

Silent night! Holy night!

All is calm, all is bright;

Round yon virgin

mother and Child,

Holy Infant, so tender and mild,

Sleep in heavenly peace,

Sleep in heavenly peace.

Joseph Mohr

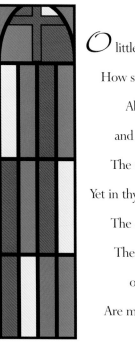

O little town of Bethlehem,

How still we see thee lie!

Above thy deep

and dreamless sleep

The silent stars go by.

Yet in thy dark streets shineth

The everlasting Light;

The hopes and fears

of all the years

Are met in thee tonight.

O holy Child of Bethlehem!

Descend to us, we pray;

Cast out our sin, and enter in;

Be born in us today.

We hear the Christmas angels

The great glad tidings tell;

O come to us, abide with us,

Our Lord Emmanuel.

Phillips Brooks

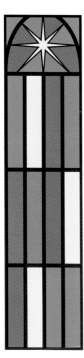

The hinge of history is on the door of a Bethlehem stable.

Ralph W. Sockman

May He who sent

the Christ Child

To earth from heaven above

Watch over you, as always,

And bless you with His love.

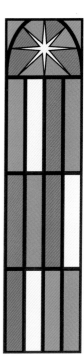

$\mathcal{G}$od loves us all so much

that he brought us all together

in hope, in love, and in peace

when He gave us the gift

of joy—Jesus!

Pay heed to the angel's

message to the shepherds,

to the heavenly announcement

of the gift of joy.

Everlasting life and endless joy

are parts of the gift

of God's Son.

Receive Him and rejoice!

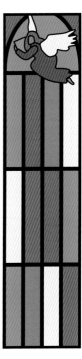

When candles glow on Christmas Eve
And snow falls glist'ning white,
I seem to see the Christmas star
That filled the world with light.

When carols ring on Christmas Eve
And bells in steeples chime,
I seem to feel the wondrous joy
Of that first Christmastime.

Norman Johnson

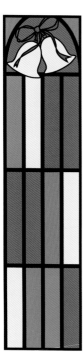

What do you see at Christmas? Same old carols. Same old tinsel. Same old light. Same old story. Same old nativity scene. But don't miss God's brand new gifts: Brand new hope. Brand new love. Brand new forgiveness. Brand new life!

God walked down

the stairs of heaven

with a Baby in his arms.

Paul Scherer

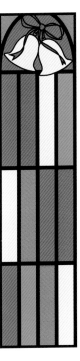

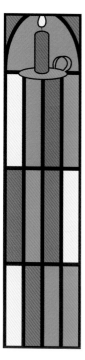

They all were looking

for a king

To slay their foes

and lift them high;

Thou cam'st, a little baby-thing

That made a woman cry.

George MacDonald

Because of Christ's

great love for us,

He became what we are

in order to make us

what He is.

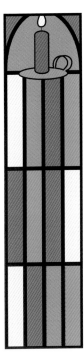

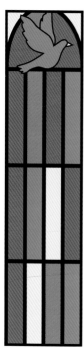

Truth can often be found

in places we would

never think to look.

After all,

God's Son was born in a stable

and laid in a manger.

Where is He

who has been born

King of the Jews?

For we saw His star in the east,

and have come to worship Him.

Matthew 2:2 NASB

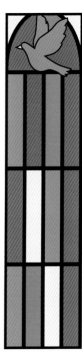

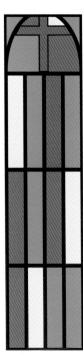

$\mathcal{I}$ wonder what would
happen if women in America
would band together
and boycott Christmas craziness
and simply worship
Him on His birthday?

Mab Graff Hoover

*C*hristmas began

in the heart of God.

It is complete only when it

reaches the heart of man.

We three kings of Orient are:

Bearing gifts we traverse afar—

Field and fountain, moor and mountain—

Following yonder star.

O star of wonder, star of night,

Star with royal beauty bright,

Westward leading, still proceeding,

Guide us to thy perfect light.

John H. Hopkins, Jr.

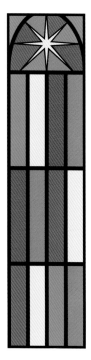

"A Christmas Prayer"

Loving Father, help us

remember the birth of Jesus,

that we may share in the

song of angels, the gladness of

the shepherds, and the worship

of the wise men. . . .

May the Christmas morning
make us happy to be Thy children,
and the Christmas evening bring
us to our beds with grateful
thoughts, forgiving and forgiven,
for Jesus' sake. Amen.

Robert Louis Stevenson

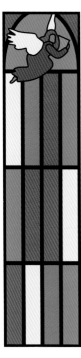

The One who inhabits eternity comes to dwell in time. The One whom none can look upon and live is delivered in a stable under the soft, indifferent gaze of cattle. The Father of all mercies puts Himself at our mercy.

Frederick Buechner

Thanks be to God

for his indescribable gift!

2 Corinthians 9:15 NIV

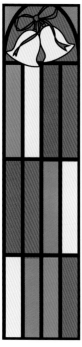

Great as he was,

Caesar Augustus is now only an

echo of ancient times, while the

name of the child he had never

heard of is spoken by millions

with reverence and love.

Walter Russell Bowie

God shook the world to its
foundations—not with a bomb,
not with an earthquake, but with
a small Baby in a manger in
Bethlehem.
The angels showered songs of
peace and good will on all.
And the world has never been
the same since.
That's the glory of Christmas!

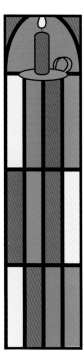

What greater message of hope and joy could the angel have brought than the good news that God had sent His Son into the world as its Savior?

Millie Stamm

This is Christmas:
not the tinsel, not the giving and
receiving; not even the carols,
but the humble heart that
receives anew the wondrous gift,
the Christ.

Frank McKibben

Three wise men that first Christmas night

Brought treasures fine and rare—

Golden coins and frankincense

And the costly spice of myrrh.

They came with love and reverence;

The Magi knelt while worshiping

In joyful adoration they

Gave thanks for the newborn King.

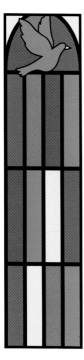

Long ago, a star guided
the Magi to the Christ child.

Wise men still seek Him.

$\mathcal{A}$nd when they saw the star,

they rejoiced exceedingly

with great joy.

Matthew 2:10 NASB

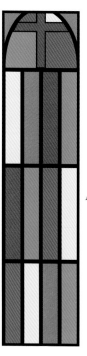

O Father,

may that Holy star

Grow every year more bright,

And send its glorious beams afar

To fill the world with light.

William Cullen Bryant

Christmas, my child,

is love in action. . . .

Every time we love,

every time we give,

it's Christmas.

Dale Evans Rogers

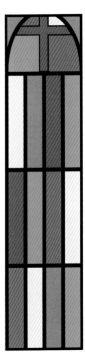

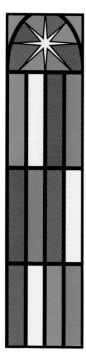

God sent his Son in peace to a world that was full of strife. This Child came bringing hope to a world that was hopeless. His life brought light to a world lost in darkness. But best of all, on Christmas, Jesus came with life, life eternal, for us all.

Good Christian men, rejoice,

With heart and soul and voice;

Give ye heed to what we say:

Jesus Christ is born today;

Ox and ass before Him bow,

And He is in the manger now.

Christ is born today!

Christ is born today!

John M. Neale

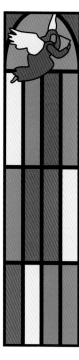

And when they had come
into the house, they saw the
young Child with Mary His
mother, and fell down and
worshiped Him. And when they
had opened their treasures,
they presented gifts to Him:
gold, frankincense, and myrrh.

Matthew 2:11 NKJV

Let us reverently bow before the holy Christ, whose innocence restores to manhood its ancient glory; and let us pray that He may be formed in us, the hope of glory.

Charles H. Spurgeon

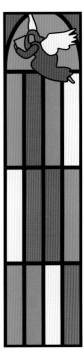

Remember while December
Brings the only Christmas Day,
In the year let there be Christmas
In the things you do and say;
Wouldn't life be worth the living
Wouldn't dreams be coming true
If we kept the Christmas spirit
All the whole year through?

Unknown

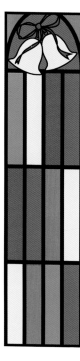

At this Christmas time, I greet you; not quite as the world sends greetings, but with profound esteem, and with the prayer that for you, now and forever, the day breaks and the shadows flee away.

Fra Giovanni

$\mathcal{R}$emember:

keeping the Christmas spirit is

good, but sharing it with others

is praiseworthy.

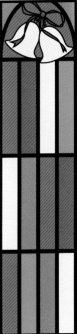

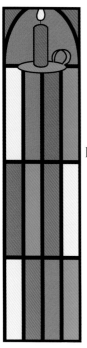

$\mathcal{A}$t this season when many

focus on the birth of Christ,

how few grasp even a little of the

magnitude of the miracle that

occurred when "the Word

was made flesh and dwelt

among us."

. . . When remembering the Babe in Bethlehem, let us not forget the Sovereign on the throne.

Alan Cairns

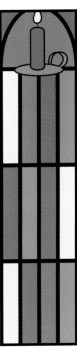

But you, Bethlehem, in the
land of Judah, are by no means
least among the rulers of Judah;
for out of you will come a ruler
who will be the shepherd of my
people Israel.

Matthew 2:6 NIV

*S*ongs of joy to celebrate Christmas did not originate until the thirteenth century when Francis of Assisi gathered people around the manger in his church to sing songs to celebrate Christ's birth. These yearly celebrations became known as "Christ's Masses"—hence our word, Christmas.

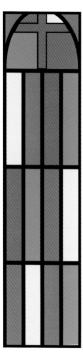

Many Christmas traditions
have their roots in the church's
celebration of Christ's birth.
Legend says that Martin Luther
cut the first Christmas tree for

his children and adorned it with

candles to symbolize the

multitude of angels that

appeared to the shepherds in

Bethlehem.

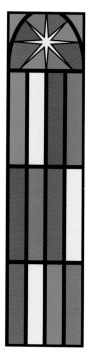

Behold, the virgin shall be

with child, and bear a Son,

and they shall call His name

"Immanuel,"

which translated means,

"God with us."

Matthew 1:23, NASB

The birth of Jesus symbolizes

that all who follow him will also

be born into new abundant

life—

created within them by the same

Holy Spirit who

created the life-saving Lord

within Mary.

Reverend Dr. James Forbes

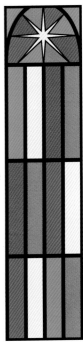

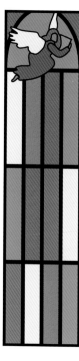

Rejoice greatly, O Daughter of Zion! Shout, Daughter of Jerusalem! See, your king comes to you, righteous and having salvation, gentle and riding on a donkey, on a colt, the foal of a donkey.

Zechariah 9:9 NIV

Christ's first coming

brought us grace;

His second coming

will bring us glory!

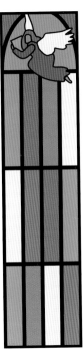